I0499905

This Journal
Belongs to

____

www.ingramcontent.com/pod-product-compliance
Lightning Source LLC
Chambersburg PA
CBHW070344220526
45467CB00001B/243
9781702600361